# A Teenager's Guide
## to Investing in the Stock Market
### Invest hard now | Play hard later

By

Luke Villermin

A Teenager's Guide to Investing in the Stock Market: Invest Hard Now | Play Hard Later by Luke Villermin

**Published by Play Later Publishing LLC**
investnowplaylater.com; facebook.com/investnowplaylater

**Copyright © 2020 Play Later Publishing LLC, Houston, TX**
Updated January 2023

**ISBN: Print 979-8-5716174-4-4**

# CONTENTS

*For all those who never let humble beginnings*
*keep them from striving for something more.*

# Disclaimer

Luke Villermin (henceforth, "the author") is not a licensed financial advisor, registered investment advisor, or registered broker-dealer. The author is not providing investment, financial, legal, or tax advice, and nothing in this book should be construed as such by you. This book should be used as an educational tool only and is not a replacement for professional investment advice.

The author and the publisher disclaim responsibility for any adverse effects resulting directly or indirectly from information contained in this book.

The full disclaimer may be found at the end of this book.

# INTRODUCTION

# YOURSELF, A MILLIONAIRE?

$2,958,497—that is the potential value of your investment account at sixty years old, if you begin saving at age twenty. Starting at age eighteen? Try $3,572,864. Age fifteen? $4,736,482. How is this possible? By putting $6,000 into a savings account each year and allowing your money to grow at a rate that matches the average performance of the stock market, you are all but guaranteed membership in the seven-figure club.

Take a special look at the difference in account balances when starting at age fifteen versus starting at age twenty—$1,777,985. A five-year delay in saving a total of $30,000 ($6,000 per year) can cost you a whopping $1.8 million at retirement.

"But wouldn't $30k buy me the car I've always wanted? I need to save up for that *now*!"

Sure, but think about what $1.8 million can buy you— a custom-built house, startup funds for your dream business, or a five-star vacation around the world. It will likely buy you all of these, and you will *still* have money left afterward.

We live in a world that values the present, but your future self will thank you for the actions you take now that will improve your life in the long term. The savings account figures I listed are to prove a point, but you do not have to save $6,000 per year to retire as a millionaire. Any little bit you can put away now will grow to a much larger number over the next few decades. All it takes is a little patience combined with the drive to actually do it.

Here is what this book is NOT—a guide to identify the next trending stock, a resource if you are looking to get rich quick, or a view into Hollywood's adrenaline-pumping portrayal of the stock market. This book's purpose is threefold:

1. Inspire you to start saving for retirement today
2. Increase your confidence in how the stock market operates
3. Provide a step-by-step road map to becoming an investor

I began investing in the stock market at fifteen years old. In that time, I have screwed up a lot, but I have also had a lot of success. In this book, I have baked up strategies that can help you win and steps to get you started, based on my own experiences. The action plan that I have created can be implemented starting today, and the stock market fundamentals I introduce will help you make your own educated decisions based on your unique situation. And of course, my goal is to keep things from getting overwhelming (which was difficult to do given all the Wall Street lingo out there).

Once you complete the steps in this book, you will be able to brag to your friends about:

- The invisible force that will make you a millionaire
- How trillion-dollar corporations are depositing their profits directly into your bank account
- Why picking money-making stocks is easier than picking a prom date

- How the cash you start investing will eventually make you more money than forty years of your future salary, combined
- Why, even as a teenager, you can produce better investing results than the average billionaire on Wall Street

It is frustratingly simple to become a millionaire, yet most people do not have the patience or discipline to ever make it. Are you okay with being average? Likely not—that is why you opened this book! More money than you can imagine lies right in front of you. You just have to keep reading and go get it.

If you invest hard now, you can play hard later.

# CHAPTER 1

## WHY IT'S IMPORTANT TO START INVESTING EARLY

S o, what will it take to become a millionaire, say, by retirement? Well, it depends entirely on when you start saving and investing. The earlier you begin, the less you have to invest. If you begin investing in the stock market at age twenty, and experience mediocre returns (throughout this book we will assume 9.7% annual growth, which is what the broader stock market has averaged since the early 1900s), you need to invest $173 per month to have $1 million in your account by age sixty. Not too bad, right?

If you begin investing at eighteen, you will need to put in only $142 per month to retire a millionaire. And if you begin at fifteen, a measly $106 is all that is needed. This is very doable.

The average American waits until they are thirty-one years old to begin saving for retirement...which means they will need to invest $522 per month to have a shot at retiring a millionaire. Better late than never, I guess? But you see in my opinion, it is way too late. These people have given up an entire decade of investing help from the world's most powerful force—compounding. Compounding shows that the time value of an investment is often much more important than even the amount of initial money invested.

To envision compounding in my day-to-day life, I like to follow what I call the "Cheeseburger Rule."

The Cheeseburger Rule is all about opportunity cost. That is, taking part in some activity or making a purchase now causes me to give up  something else—a lost opportunity. If I decide to go out for dinner with friends and buy a cheeseburger, it costs me around $20 (after the loaded fries and added milkshake, of course). But this cheeseburger has future value, because if I instead *invested* $20 today, how much would it be worth, say, in forty years? Remember that average 9.7% annual return? By foregoing the opportunity to invest my $20 at 9.7% for forty years, I am actually paying $890.23 for this cheeseburger today. By going out with friends now, I am giving up nearly $900 in the future. Is this a trade I am willing to make? Maybe, because everyone must eat. However, think about things like this in your daily life, and you will spend money—and save money—differently.

At your age, giving up the latest pair of shoes to, instead, invest money for retirement is a concept that many around you will struggle to comprehend. There is peer pressure all around you encouraging you to spend your money. Well, I am sure your friends will one day look great in their new shoes while standing on *your* yacht! If you want financial security later in life, this is the proven method to get there. Heck—hand your friends this book once you are finished and get them to join the millionaire mindset themselves!

To give a more detailed example of the invisible force of compounding, consider a scenario in which you are the star quarterback of your high school football team. To play your best, you like to have a sports drink before and after practices and games. You currently drink 100 sports drinks a month (that's a lot of electrolytes). However, your coach, who really wants to keep you from getting dehydrated throughout the season, comes to you and says he will increase the number of sports drinks he gives you by 10% each month, for the next six months.

Okay, so a 10% increase of 100 sports drinks would be ten more sports drinks, right? You may think your next six months look like this:

Month 0 (starting amount): 100 sports drinks

Month 1: 100 + 10 = 110 sports drinks

Month 2: 100 + 10 + 10 = 120 sports drinks

Month 3: 100 + 10 + 10 + 10 = 130 sports drinks

Month 4: 100 + 10 + 10 + 10 + 10 = 140 sports drinks

Month 5: 100 + 10 + 10 + 10 + 10 + 10 = 150 sports drinks

Month 6: 100 + 10 + 10 + 10 + 10 + 10 + 10 = 160 sports drinks

You are getting a total of sixty extra sports drinks by the end of six months. Yet, that is not how compounding works. You do not just get an extra 10% of your *initial* 100 sports drinks month after month—you get an extra 10% of your *total* amount of sports drinks every month, including the extra that you got the prior month:

Month 0 (starting amount) = 100 sports drinks

Month 1: 100 + (100 x 10%) = 110 sports drinks

Month 2: 110 + (110 x 10%) = 121 sports drinks

Month 3: 121 + (121 x 10%) = 133 sports drinks

Month 4: 133 + (133 x 10%) = 146 sports drinks

Month 5: 146 + (146 x 10%) = 161 sports drinks

Month 6: 161 + (161 x 10%) = 177 sports drinks

With compounding, you get a total of seventy-seven extra sports drinks by the end of six months. Substantially better than sixty, right? And guess what—the longer you allow compounding to occur, the greater the impact. If our star quarterback goes on to play in college, or maybe even professionally, and the consumption of sports drinks continues to grow 10% each month, the effects of compounding become even more profound. If this continues for ten years (120 months), you will somehow have to find a way to drink 10,197,998 sports drinks per month by the end of it.

Similarly, if your money is invested in the stock market, it will experience compounding growth. Your money makes you money, and then that extra money makes you even more money, and then that money makes money, which makes money, which makes more money, and this goes on and on and on—it is an exponential increase! Now, it is important to note, returns in the stock market are not guaranteed. You can keep your money in a savings account and earn interest—where the bank pays you to save your money with them so that they can loan it out to others—but this interest is rarely more than 1%. The good thing is that your balance will never go down—unless you spend it of course. Yes, in a savings account your money will be compounding, but at a much lower rate. If you invest in the stock market, your balance may go down in the short term. Still, the stock market has averaged close to 10% annual growth since the early 1900s. There are some years it goes up, and some years it goes down, but in the long run, over time, the stock market goes up.

I have included a graphic to give you a taste of just how powerful compounding returns can be (figure 1). This graph depicts a hypothetical investment account in which the owner saves $6,000 per year, beginning at age eighteen. Investments in the owner's account earn 9.7% annually. Because of compounding, the total interest earned quickly surpasses the amount of money that the investor ever even puts into the account. This is truly putting money to work!

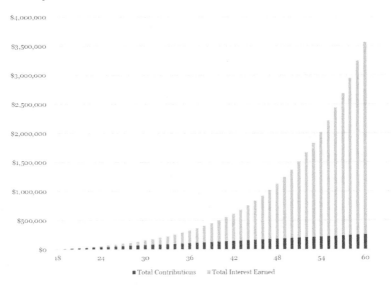

Figure 1: Compounding at Work (assuming 9.7% annual return)

Now, you are probably thinking that this is all fine and dandy, but there are other things on your mind: tests to study for, club soccer practice, band rehearsal, shopping, college applications to complete. Not to mention the money you need to save to buy a car, pay tuition, and just hang out with friends. Although many of these are important and natural things to focus on as a teenager, what if I told you that three actions alone have the potential to impact the second half of your life even *more so* than whatever university you get into, the degree you seek there, and the job you get afterward? Those three important actions are quite simple really:

1. Open a retirement account and regularly add money to it.
2. Use that money to invest in the stock market and generate compounded returns.
3. Do not take out any money until you retire.

"Woah...retirement! Luke, you're saying that I need to use the little money that I *do* have to save for something that is over *forty years* in the future!?"

That is exactly what I am saying. Scrape up all your spare change, find a job, and buckle up for the most "adult" thing you have accomplished since you passed your driver's ed test. There is so much to lose by not starting ASAP.

This is a call to action. A rallying cry. Time is of the essence. If you wait to start saving until after you graduate, after you find a job, after you pay off student loans, after the down payment on the house—you'll find yourself only starting to think about retirement at thirty-one years old, like the average American, and you will retire with $2,543,820 less in your account. I will write that out again—by not opening a retirement account and purchasing stock today, you could be taking 2.5 million dollars straight from the pocket of your future self (figure 2).

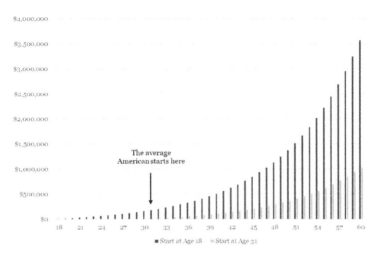

Figure 2: Investors Starting at Age 18 vs. 31
(assuming 9.7% annual return; $6,000 annual contribution)

To put this into perspective, I will state it a different way. The cash you start saving now will eventually be worth more money than *forty years* of your future salary, *combined*. The average annual salary in the US is $60,000 per year, so it would take almost four decades of working and pocketing 100% of your income to reach $2.5 million. Thus, is the magic of compounding, and the importance of starting early.

Come on, get up. Off the bed. Go look into your mirror. Who do you see looking back at you?

I'll tell you who—a future multimillionaire. You can live an average life, well within your comfort zone, living paycheck to paycheck like the people you see around you. Or, you can break out of the mold, start working hard now, and secure your financial freedom. Starting to save and invest early is one of the greatest favors you will ever do for your future self. Do not let valuable time go to waste.

In the next chapter, we lay down some investing fundamentals and define more of the lingo. Congratulations, you are well on your way to the seven-figure club.

## Things to Think About

1. Would you be happy having your parents' financial situation as your own, once you reach their age? Are they good role models when it comes to finances, or do you think you can do better? If your parents had more money right now, would their lives be easier?

2. How often do you consciously think about the cost of something before you buy it?

3. Have you ever not done something correctly, only to regret it later? How did it make you feel once you realized?

4. If you have a regular savings account at a bank, what percentage interest is your money currently earning?

# CHAPTER 2

# STOCK MARKET BASICS

How are your grades looking in algebra? Or precalculus? I do not care, because you do not need to be good at math to become a millionaire (please don't tell your math teacher). As proclaimed by the National Financial Educators Council, only 19% of students will use high-school-level algebra in their eventual job, but 100% of students will benefit from financial literacy, which includes solid investment knowledge. Next time your parents ask you about your latest math test, talk to them about what you learned in this chapter instead. I will show you *how* to invest in a later chapter. First, it is important to know the basics.

Just as you require money to go to college and build your future, corporations require money (a.k.a. capital) to build their businesses. To raise this capital, they sell fractions of themselves to the public—shares of stock. A share of stock represents a "piece of the pie" of a whole company. The stock "market" is a venue for trading shares of stock. Well-known stock markets include the New York Stock Exchange (NYSE), National Association of Securities Dealers Automated Quotations (NASDAQ), and London Stock Exchange (LSE). To buy a portion, or share, of a company, there must be another person on the other side of the transaction to sell it to you. Likewise, to sell a share of stock, someone must be willing to buy it. When there are more "buyers" than "sellers," the stock price rises—the simple law of supply and demand. People are willing to pay more and more for ownership of the company (usually because they believe that it will increase in value). And vice versa—when there are more "sellers" than "buyers," the stock price drops. Hundreds of millions of shares of stock are traded every day. Well, every Monday through Friday, excluding Federal holidays, of course.

Now, there are two primary ways that being a shareholder (stock owner) can pay off:

1. An increase in the price of the stock

2. Income generated by dividend payments

As the value of a company rises, the price of the stock you own increases, and at some point you will (hopefully) be able to sell your shares for more money than you paid to purchase them.

Dividend payments are a little more involved. Have you ever received an allowance? An allowance is when you receive money from your parents just for existing. That is basically what a dividend is—a corporation's payment to shareholders just for existing. Dividend payments are quarterly payouts (every three months) of a company's earnings, deposited straight into your account. The more shares you hold, the more dividends you will receive. Larger, more stable corporations are the most frequent issuers of dividend payments, and they often increase their dividend payments annually.

As an example, say you own 100 shares of Verizon Communications, Inc. As of this writing, the quarterly shareholder dividend payment is $0.62 per share. How much will you get paid, just for owning 100 shares of Verizon stock?

$0.62 per share x 100 shares = $62 per dividend payment

$62 per payment x 4 payments per year = $248 per year

$248 per year, just for owning shares in the company! Easy money, right? It gets even better, though. Remember, you also make money if the price of each *share* increases, as shown in figure 3. If you bought 100 shares of Verizon stock on December 31, 2009, you would have paid around $18.59 per share, for a total of $1,859. Ten years later, on December 31, 2019, your initial investment would now be worth $5,876, considering both the increase in share price and reinvested dividend payouts—an annual return of 12.2%. You read that right, you can automatically reinvest your dividend payments to buy more shares, and therefore receive even *more* dividend payments (this is a very common thing, and is easy to do—more on this later). Compounding at work!

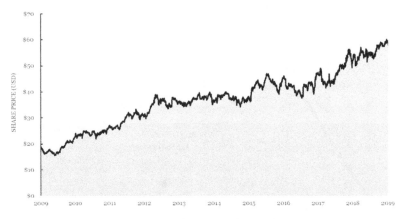

Figure 3: Verizon (VZ) Stock Performance
(excluding dividends)

Now, as alluded to earlier, the stock market is not always this rosy. There is risk involved with all investments, and out of all the available types, stocks are considered on the riskier side (figure 4). You could technically lose all your invested money if a company goes bankrupt, and many past investors have. Still, there are ways to mitigate this risk. It is actually encouraged to have a healthy amount of risk in your investment portfolio—especially for investors on the younger side—because as your "risk" increases, your potential "reward" increases as well (more on this later). Most experts recommend that people have an investment strategy that naturally reduces risk when approaching retirement by spreading out their collection of investments across stocks, bonds, annuities, real estate investment trusts (REITs), etc. This is called diversification. However, we are ignoring bonds, annuities, and REITs in this book because the approaches here are designed for someone in the early years of their life. A young person can ride the ups and downs of the stock market easier than someone five years from retirement. For young investors, taking on the extra risk now will likely result in greater rewards in the long run. This is referred to as taking on a more "aggressive" investment strategy. We will touch on this in more detail in chapter 4.

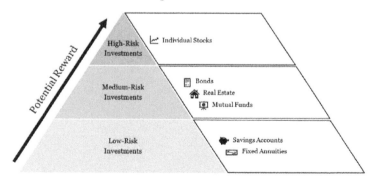

Figure 4: Investment Relative-Risk Pyramid

Further to this point, diversification will allow you to spread out your risk. You have likely heard the phrase "don't put all your eggs in one basket." If your entire investment portfolio consists of one stock, and it drops and goes bankrupt, your portfolio is gone! Instead, try to invest in a variety of companies in a variety of industries. Hopefully, you will have more winners than losers. In chapter 4, we will discuss more strategies that optimize this.

To recap our key takeaways:

1. When you buy a share of stock, you become partial owner of that company—you are invested in its future!
2. Owning stock can make you money in two ways—an increase in share price and dividend payments.

You may be thinking, "...well I read this whole chapter on the stock market and investing basics, but I still don't know how to pick the right stock..." That is okay, because you will likely not be picking most of your portfolio yourself. Study after study has shown that you will do much better by investing in a preallocated, diversified portfolio of companies that track the overall market. Sound boring? Maybe. Yet, I still do not think retiring a multimillionaire is boring.

Before you begin investing, we have one more thing to touch on: taxes. Or the lack thereof. Up to this point in your life, you have not had to think about taxes very much. If only that could continue! When you sell stocks for a profit you incur a "capital gains" tax, which is collected by the government. However, there is a way to avoid losing your hard-invested dollars to taxes if you save and invest through the correct account type. We will dive right into this next, in chapter 3.

## Things to Think About

1. How much patience do you have? Would you be able to stomach watching your account balance go up and down as your stocks' prices change?
2. Looking around at the items around you—your shoes, phone, television, car. How many are sold by a public company that is traded in the stock market? If you buy stock in that company and it pays out dividends, could you potentially be getting paid every time someone else buys that same product?

# CHAPTER 3

# UNCLE SAM WANTS YOUR MONEY, BUT HE ALSO WANTS YOU TO SAVE AND INVEST

F ranklin D. Roosevelt once said, "Taxes are the dues that we pay for the privileges of membership in an organized society." I agree with FDR, and taxes will always be here. Sometimes the government cuts us some slack, though—in this case, to encourage people to save. Americans have issues saving and investing for retirement, and many people find themselves working late into life because they cannot afford to stop getting a paycheck.  To help combat this, the US government passed the Taxpayer Relief Act of 1997 and established what is known as a Roth Individual Retirement Account (Roth IRA).

## The Roth IRA

A Roth IRA allows you to add a certain amount of money to an account each year, and then when you eventually retire, you do not have to pay taxes on any of the money you take out (which is *huge*). The initial money that you deposit inside of the Roth is called a "contribution," and you can transfer contributions directly from your primary bank account as often as you like. One day, when you eventually sell your investments, you will generate "earnings." Earnings are the profits you make in the stock market, on top of your initial investment. In a Roth, you can typically pick from a wide variety of investments to put your cash to work—it's your choice!

As mentioned earlier, you are one day going to have to pay taxes. You will pay taxes as a percentage of your job income, taxes on your home, taxes on things you buy, and the list goes on and on. You also must pay taxes on earnings in the stock market. Again, this is called a "capital gains" tax. Say you allow your money to grow year after year for a few decades, and then you withdraw from your account to buy a vacation home on the beach. Well, depending on the amount you withdraw, you could be required to pay over *40%* of your earnings straight to the government. Poof—gone! That beach house is now half the size you were planning.

Before you get too discouraged, allow me to explain the Roth IRA in more detail. As a Roth IRA account owner, you are exempt from paying capital gains taxes at disbursement (retirement, beginning at age 59 1/2). The contributions into your account will be added only *after* you pay income taxes on them (a.k.a. "after-tax contributions"). In other words, you get the taxes out of the way now, so that you can reap the rewards of your compounded investments later. Once in your account and invested in the market, it can compound for 10, 20, 30+ years, *tax free*. I do not know about you, but I would much prefer to pay my tax percentage on a small number of dollars now, rather than the millions I will have later!

How about we use two sisters as an example. Anna and Jane are both hard-working teenagers with a desire to save big now so that they can take it easy in life later. After the school day ends, they go to work. During the summer, they work. They work as many hours as they can get. Starting at age eighteen, both Anna and Jane are each able to save and invest $6,000. They do this annually until retirement at age sixty. Throughout their lives, both earn an average salary of $60,000 per year, the US median income (which impacts how much you pay in taxes). Anna makes her investments through a Roth IRA account. Jane, however, is a little clumsy; she neglects to put her money in a tax-advantaged account like a Roth and instead just opens a standard investment account. This is a horrible mistake! Assuming an average annual return of 9.7%, Jane will retire with $1.69 million *less* than Anna—all because of the taxes she will owe to the government (figure 5). Make sure that you open the correct account type!

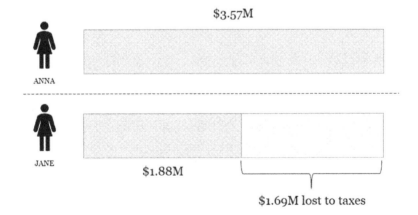

Figure 5: Hypothetical Roth IRA (Anna) vs. Standard Taxable Account (Jane) at Retirement

It is worth noting that there are other account types that people use for retirement savings: the Traditional IRA, and the 401(k).

## The Traditional IRA

While a Roth IRA allows for *after-tax* contributions, a Traditional IRA allows for *pre-tax* contributions. This means that whatever money you put into a Traditional IRA you can deduct from your income taxes for that year; however, unlike the Roth, you must pay taxes on all withdrawals once you retire, as it is treated as income. In summary, a Roth IRA allows you to enjoy more money in the future, while a Traditional IRA allows you to enjoy more money today. It is widely accepted that a Roth IRA is the way to go if you will be in a higher tax bracket once you retire and begin to take withdrawals. As a teenager, you fit the bill for this description (you will likely get raises throughout your working career, thus placing you in a higher income tax bracket at retirement).

## The 401(k)

You do not have a 401(k), nor do any of your friends, but the adults in your life have likely brought it up in conversation before. What is it? Well, all things considered, a 401(k) is not very different from an IRA—in fact, they can also be set up either as a "Traditional" 401(k) or a "Roth" 401(k). It is also an account meant for retirement savings and investments. You can contribute up to a certain amount of your earnings to it each year, invest it, and then begin taking money out at retirement. Aside from some nuanced taxation differences, the primary distinguishing attribute of a 401(k), versus an IRA, is that the 401(k) is "employer sponsored." One day farther down the road, you may find yourself working for a company that offers an employee 401(k) retirement plan. Many employers want to encourage their employees to save (more savings = better financial security = less stress = happier employees), so they offer a "match." For example, if you allocate 3% of your paycheck each week to your 401(k), your employer matches 3% on *top* of your contribution, so that 6% total is being added to the account. Make sure to take advantage of this option if you have it, or once you work for a company that does—a company match is an automatic, and immediate, 100% return on your investment!

## Roth IRA Qualifications and Requirements

Okay, so we have determined that a Roth IRA account type is best suited for you—again, primarily because you are starting to invest so early. The specific rules applied to Roth IRAs have changed over time. Check irs.gov to get the latest, but here are some account requirements to consider:

1.  The maximum annual contribution limit for a Roth IRA (as of 2023) is $6,500. You are not allowed to deposit more than the maximum limit into your account, for a given tax year. This number is usually adjusted up over time to account for inflation.

2.  There is a maximum income limit, over which you must phase out of Roth IRA contributions. As of 2023, you cannot earn more than $153,000 per year and still deposit money into a Roth IRA. This requirement is not difficult to meet for most teenagers!

LUKE VILLERMIN

3. If you withdraw *contributions* before age 59 1/2, you pay no tax or penalty. However, withdrawing *earnings* before age 59 1/2 can mean you owe income tax and a ~10% penalty.

4. There is no minimum age to qualify for a Roth IRA.

5. The money deposited into a Roth IRA must be *earned income.*

Ah, see there it is. The sore point.

"You mean I can't put in all of grandma's birthday money that I've been saving up?"

Unfortunately, you cannot. A good number of people may stop reading this book now and never consider saving for retirement again until that ripe old age of thirty-one years, the American average. The idea of having to get a job just to open a retirement account may not seem worth it—it simply requires too much effort. It may appear that too much sacrifice is required to get a job and earn income, solely to qualify for a Roth IRA account. If you are feeling disheartened by this concept, please refresh your determination with all the dollar signs I showed you in chapter 1.

Fortunately, you can get creative here, and you might be relieved to know that self-employment counts. According to the Internal Revenue Service (IRS), earned income is defined as "wages, salaries, tips, and net earnings from self-employment."[1] Payments for doing lawn care or babysitting count as earned income, and thus qualify for contribution into your Roth IRA account. Again, you cannot

_____

[1] Ultimately, it is you, the taxpayer, who must prove to the IRS the presence of compensation or "earned income" for IRA contribution purposes (if they ask). If you are unsure of what qualifies as earned income, you should seek professional tax advice.

26

put in more than was earned. If you earn $2,125 for the year by cutting grass all summer, you can contribute up to $2,125 to your IRA. Obviously, this requirement is a limiting factor for young savers. Put in what you can, but maxing out is ideal.

Need other job ideas? Most fast-food restaurants start hiring at age sixteen, so get off the couch and start applying. There is no shame in flipping patties now so that you can be  worth millions of dollars later. Remember that Cheeseburger Rule? The logic can be applied to this scenario too. If you make $8 in one hour and invest it in the market at age sixteen, it could be worth over $515 down the line. Making $500+ for one hour of work—as a teenager! Think about that on the job, and I bet you will find yourself flipping patties with a bit more pep in your step. Get yourself a job and invest as much as you can into your new Roth IRA. Your future self will not regret it. Figure 6 may provide you with ideas.

| Self-Employment | Through a Part-Time Job |
| --- | --- |
| Do yard work | Restaurants |
| Pet sit | Movie theatres |
| Babysit | Pizza delivery |
| Tutor others in your favorite subject | Retail stores |
| Freelance photography | Grocery stores |
| Walk dogs | Sports referee |
| Clean houses | Golf caddy |
| Shovel snow | Landscaping businesses |
| Scoop dog poop | Bowling alleys |
| Paint fences | Summer camps |
| Create and sell art | Car wash |
| Build websites for local businesses | Pool lifeguard / swim instructor |

Figure 6: Ways to Earn Income as a Teenager

Also remember, if you begin investing at age eighteen, you will need to save and invest only $142 per month to retire at age sixty with $1,000,000 in your account. If you earn $7/hour, that means you only need to work five hours each week to become a millionaire. I'm not making this stuff up. It is as easy as one Saturday shift delivering pizzas.

## Things to Think About

1. How hard are you willing to work now so that you can have a more satisfying life later?

2. What do you currently spend your free time doing? How much "future money" is this time costing you (think Cheeseburger Rule) by not using it to work and earn investment money, instead?

3. What are some things your friends do to earn money? Do they have any contacts that could help you get a job?

4. If you have already made money from working a job this year, how much total have you made? How much of this could you afford to put into a Roth IRA as an investment?

5. You likely hear the adults in your life complain about having to pay taxes, but do they know about the tax-advantaged properties of a Roth IRA that were mentioned in this chapter? Are they unknowingly losing some of their hard-earned money to taxes while they try to save for retirement?

# CHAPTER 4

# DECIDING WHAT TO INVEST IN

D eciding what to invest in is like picking your date for prom. There are many candidates out there, but only a few of them are a potential match—some may bail on you, and never even show up! That sounds like a big risk to put yourself through. What is the best method for scoring a great prom date and locking in a fun night? Well, cast a wide net. Narrow down a list of your top, say, ten candidates, and ask them all out. Some will say no, but since you *diversified*, you will likely walk away with at least one winner.

I see no way this could go wrong...(for the record, I personally always found that I had more available stocks to choose from than potential prom dates).

Okay, maybe you should not treat every aspect of your personal life like you do your stock portfolio, but I hope you get the point. Some of the investments you make will be losers—all investors have them. However, if you do your research and narrow down your pool, then invest a portion of your total funds by purchasing stock in multiple companies, you will reduce your risk and increase your odds of coming out ahead.

## Risk vs. Reward

As touched on earlier, all investments come with risk. Risk refers to the likelihood that you will lose money on an investment. The riskier the investment, the higher the potential reward; the safer the investment, the lower the potential reward. It is a trade-off.

For example, if you want the reward of scoring a date to prom, you have to risk a lot of rejection. If you want the reward of becoming a professional football player, you have to risk getting seriously injured. If you want the reward of becoming a stock market millionaire, you have to risk losing some of your money.

Successful investors find a key balance between risk and reward—usually through the "wide net" tactic of diversification.

## Implementing Diversification

A properly diversified portfolio is made up of investments across all industries of all sizes. This limits your risk while still providing plenty of upside for your money to grow. While you can always pick out and invest in many different companies, one at a time, there are two mechanisms for diversifying your portfolio *without* having to buy shares of each separate stock yourself: mutual funds and exchange-traded funds (ETFs).

Have you ever gotten a box of chocolates for Valentine's day? You know what I am talking about, those heart-shaped trays that usually contain a wide variety of flavors for you to try. That is how mutual funds and ETFs can be considered—a package of many different stocks, all wrapped up for you with a bow on top. We will go into further detail on how easy it is to become a stock investor with these two sweet deals; just try not to get a sugar rush.

## Mutual Funds

Mutual funds are a collection of stocks that a banker on Wall Street researches and selects for you. When "retail" (nonprofessional) investors like you and me buy into a mutual fund, our cash is all pooled together. Then, the money manager selects which investments to make. The average mutual fund holds over 100 different companies, so naturally, your investment is very diversified. Mutual funds have different goals (which are stated in their "prospectus"— basically just a summary of their investment strategy).

Some seek to focus on capital gains (they buy stocks at low prices and sell them at higher prices), while others focus on companies that pay out high dividends. Some mutual funds focus on certain industries (technology, energy, real estate, consumer products, industrials, telecommunication, aerospace, defense, etc.). Some mutual funds do not even invest in the stock market but instead tracking bonds—which are loans to companies or to the government—and other lower-risk securities.

Aside from some minor differences, you will get a return on your mutual fund investment in the same two ways as if you just owned stock in one company:

1.  If the fund sells shares of stock that have increased in price, the profits will be passed on to investors in the form of a distribution.
2.  Dividend payouts are passed on to investors in the form of a distribution.

However, if the fund holdings increase in price but the fund manager decides not to sell them, then the mutual fund's shares *themselves* increase in price—and thus you can then sell your entire investment to someone else for a profit.

Sounds great, right? You sit back while someone else puts your money to work.

However, one thing you should be extra wary of when investing into mutual funds: fees. These fees are referred to as the fund's "expense ratio." As a rule, the more actively managed a fund is (when the manager tries to outperform the broader stock market), the higher the fees they will charge. Fees are charged to your investment as a percentage, and on average, they will be in the 0.5%–1.0% range. In the long run, these can start to add up and will eat into the money you make.

Here are some well-known mutual funds:[2]

- Fidelity Investments' Magellan Fund (FMAGX): Perhaps the most renowned actively managed mutual fund because of its long history
- Vanguard Total Stock Market Index Fund (VTSAX): Covers the entire US stock market
- Fidelity Contrafund Fund (FCNTX): Actively managed portfolio of large, undervalued companies with strong earnings growth
- Schwab International Index Fund (SWISX): Tracks non-US companies across Japan, Australia, Germany, France, Switzerland, and the United Kingdom

## Exchange-Traded Funds

ETFs are a very similar concept to mutual funds, in that they represent a broader group of investments. However, in contrast to most mutual funds' active management, ETFs are *passively* managed. ETFs are set up by the folks on Wall Street to track an underlying index (basket of stocks) based on some common criteria, but then they just let them ride. There may be a few tweaks or rebalancing in the fund here and there, but there is very little "cherry picking" going on because they are trying to simply *match* the market, not outperform it. As a result, most ETF fees are lower than mutual fund fees, but they still do exist because there is some cost to operating and managing the fund.

---

[2] Please note that I am not encouraging investment in any of these securities, merely providing examples. Please perform your own research to make educated financial decisions.

Here are some of the most popular ETFs:[3]

- SPDR S&P 500 (SPY): Tracks the S&P 500 Index, the 500 largest public companies in the US.
- SPDR Dow Jones Industrial Average (DIA): Tracks the thirty stocks of the Dow Jones Industrial Average, which aims to represent the American economy
- Invesco QQQ (QQQ): Tracks the Nasdaq 100, which is mostly technology stocks
- iShares Russell 2000 (IWM): Tracks the Russell 2000 small-cap index, representing 2,000 of the smallest public companies in the US.

You may have noticed the word "index" listed in the names of some mutual funds, as well as ETFs. An index shows the hypothetical performance of a chosen basket of stocks, usually the broader market in some fashion. An "index fund" is an actual legal entity that is designed to track an index, and these funds can be structured as mutual funds or ETFs. Index funds are generally less actively managed, which in turn will usually result in lower fees. Figure 7 places mutual funds and ETFs side-by-side for a clear comparison of the two.

---

[3] Please note that I am not encouraging investment in any of these securities, merely providing examples. Please perform your own research to make educated financial decisions.

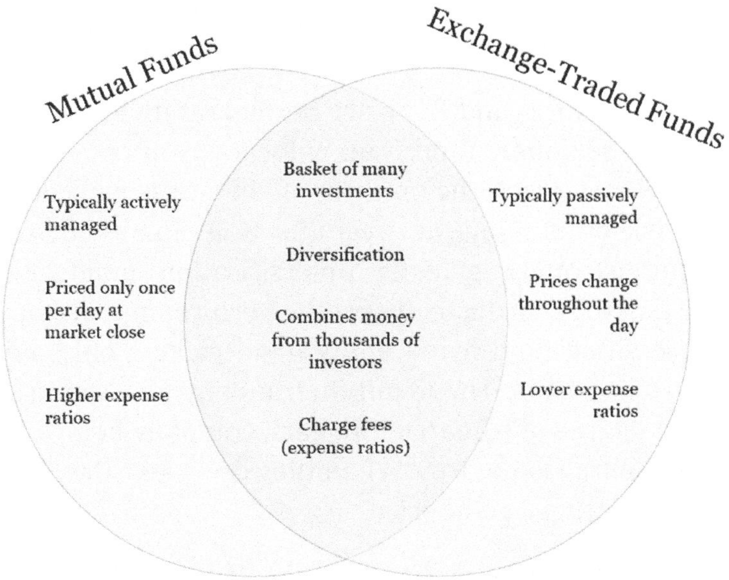

**Mutual Funds**

**Exchange-Traded Funds**

Typically actively managed

Priced only once per day at market close

Higher expense ratios

Basket of many investments

Diversification

Combines money from thousands of investors

Charge fees (expense ratios)

Typically passively managed

Prices change throughout the day

Lower expense ratios

Figure 7: A Comparison of Funds

There are many mutual fund and ETF screeners available online to help you choose your approach. You can search by name, category, or industry and do a side-by-side comparison of historical performance, top holdings (which companies they are most heavily invested in), and expense ratios across similar funds. There are also several rating agencies that rank funds on all of these variables and present them in a way that is easy to compare. When you are researching mutual funds and/or ETFs to decide what to invest in, remember to look for these big three items, which will all be clearly stated on any fund summary page:

1. Historical Performance (what has been the average annual return of the fund over the past 5, 10, 15+ years)
2. Expense Ratio (what percentage of your money will be lost to fees each year)

3. Diversification (what variety of companies is built into the fund)

Mutual funds and ETFs are both great investment vehicles for beginners (and frankly for investors of all ages) because they track the returns of the stock market and limit risk by building in diversification. Some, however, feel quite strongly against a "diversification" mindset and know that they can instead beat the performance of a heavily diversified fund by carefully hand-picking only a few stocks to invest in. They limit their risk by performing the highest degree of research into each company before they begin to purchase shares. When they do invest, they know they are getting a good price.

"Diversification is a protection against ignorance. It makes very little sense to those who know what they are doing." —Warren Buffet

## Value Investing and the Portfolio Focus Strategy

Have you ever bought a new pair of jeans during a 50%-off flash sale? Well, believe it or not, there are essentially "sales" in the stock market as well. Seeking out companies at bargain prices is commonly referred to as value investing. Value investing is like buying a discounted stock at dirt-cheap prices and betting that eventually the rest of the investing community will catch on and drive the share price higher, closer to its true value. This is tied primarily to expectations on the future earnings potential of the company, as well as its financial stability.

Warren Buffet, one of the world's most renowned value investors, is an advocate for the "Portfolio Focus Strategy," which, unlike a diversification strategy, seeks to select and own a handful of companies with very strong fundamentals—and then hold on to them indefinitely. For example, Coca-Cola was one of Buffet's most successful investments. He first purchased shares of the company back in 1988 when the stock price was struggling, and got a fantastic bargain. As of this writing, he still owns the investment, and it is now worth over $18 billion, an increase of over 1,300%!

If you want to follow the Portfolio Focus Strategy instead of investing into a mutual fund or ETF, you will need to research and select stocks on your own. In this investment strategy, you are your own money manager!

This may seem intimidating at first, but you will likely get the hang of it in no time. Many amateur investors just throw all of their money in one stock because the company is trending on social media, or because their cousin told them about it, or because the share price has been rocketing upward all week. Would you take a college entrance exam without first studying for it? Do not buy a stock without first researching it. The extra effort is worth it. Next, we will go into some beginner metrics that are commonly used to examine the fundamental health of a company.

CHECK IN: How are you feeling right now? I am about to go into detail on how to choose your own stocks. If you feel like you have a good grasp on mutual funds and ETFs, but adding more information would be overwhelming, I would encourage you to skip over to chapter 5. Follow the steps there to open your new account, and then split your savings amongst one or more ETFs and mutual funds. I would much rather you enter the stock market now with one of the preceding strategies, than get overwhelmed and never start at all. There is no shame in getting your toes wet with an ETF or mutual fund before jumping into the more complicated strategies!

Okay, continuing onward. Here are some common metrics that you will come across when you research individual stocks. This is essential vocabulary for a value investor.

**Market Cap**—a measure of the overall size of the company, in terms of total dollar value. In general, the larger the market capitalization, the "bigger" the company, and the less likely the company is to fail, or go bankrupt. A company with a larger market cap will often experience slower growth than one with a smaller market cap; as a result, companies with a larger market cap often payout dividends to compensate investors. The investing community sorts publicly traded companies by size, as follows:

- Large-cap = $10 billion or more
- Mid-cap = $2 billion to $10 billion
- Small-cap = $300 million to $2 billion
- Micro-cap = less than $300 million

When you are looking at a stock, how can you determine its market cap? Most online investment websites will list this metric front and center on the stock summary page. You can also calculate it yourself with this equation:

Market Capitalization = Current Market Price of Share x Number of Total Outstanding Shares

"Total Outstanding Shares" refers to the total number of shares investors currently own. Therefore, a company's market cap can go up or down in two ways: (1) the stock price changes, or (2) the company "issues" more shares of stock to raise money or "buys" some shares back to increase shareholder value. The market cap of a company is always changing. Usually, the larger a company's market cap, the less risky it is, and the more stable it is as an investment. Looking at market cap is also useful when you are trying to size up how valuable the public perceives a company to be.

**Earnings per Share (EPS)**—one of the most common fundamentals to look at when evaluating the health of a company is its earnings. EPS tells an investor how much profit their company is bringing in, on every share of stock that they own. The definition of "earnings" can get kind of complicated, but the simplest formula for calculating this is:

Earnings Per Share = Profits / Total Outstanding Shares

The period for these values is usually on an annual basis (looking at four quarters of earnings). A company with an EPS that increases over time is usually more enticing than one with a decreasing EPS. You can view graphs of a company's EPS over time with a quick online search.

**P/E Ratio**—not to be confused with gym class, the P/E stands for price-to-earnings ratio. Many investors use this ratio to determine the relative value of a company, which allows you to conclude whether the company's stock price is "overvalued" or "undervalued." Because P/E is a ratio, it allows you to compare "apples-to-apples" between companies in a similar industry (tech, consumer goods, etc.). At heart, the P/E ratio shows how much an investor is willing to pay for each dollar of the company's earnings. If the P/E ratio of a stock is currently 15, this indicates that an investor is willing to pay $15 for $1 of current earnings. A higher ratio shows that investors are okay with paying a higher price to own the stock today because of future growth expectations. The formula for calculating this is as follows:

P/E Ratio = Stock Price / EPS

Historically, the average P/E ratio for all the companies in the S&P 500 (the 500 largest public companies in the US) has ranged from 13 to 15. Generally speaking, a P/E above this range may indicate that a stock is overvalued, while a lower P/E may indicate that a stock is undervalued and has been overlooked by other investors.

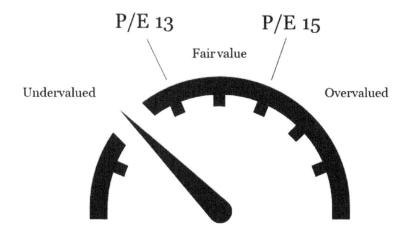

As mentioned, these metrics (and many, many more) can be easily found on any online investing website. Simply type in the stock symbol (abbreviation for the company, also called the "ticker") into the search bar and you will find a graph plotting the recent share price over time, as well as a chart listing the market cap, EPS, and P/E ratio, as starred in figure 8.

**The Coca-Cola Company (KO)**
NYSE Delayed Price

**48.21** -1.45 (-2.92%)
At close: 4:00PM EDT     Summary   Charts   News   Analyst Research   Earnings   Fundamentals

| | | | | |
|---|---|---|---|---|
| Previous Close | 49.66 | Market Cap | 207.083B | |
| Open | 49.73 | Beta | 0.55 | |
| Bid | 0.00 x 1200 | P/E | 22.74x | |
| Ask | 0.00 x 1100 | EPS | 2.12 | |
| Day's Range | 48.17 – 49.92 | Earnings Date | Oct 16, 2020 | |
| 52 Week Range | 36.27 – 60.13 | Forward Dividend & Yield | 1.64 (3.30%) | |
| Volume | 14,883,777 | Ex-Dividend Date | Sep 14, 2020 | |
| Avg. Volume | 15,415,414 | 1 Yr Target Est. | 53.90 | |

Figure 8: Stock Summary Page Mockup

## Qualitative Factors for Evaluating a Company

Whew. Now that we have gotten through the equations, you have a good foundation in the *quantitative* factors (numbers) that go into evaluating a company, but there are also more *qualitative* factors (not numbers) for an investor to consider. These are a little less tangible but include things such as the business model (how they make money), the management (CEO), and competitive advantages (patented products or influential brand names).

For example, take another look at The Coca-Cola Company (KO). In addition to the quantitative factors in figure 8, you must consider its brand image to perform a more complete analysis. Almost every person in the world recognizes Coca-Cola, and this is a huge factor in what makes the company so valuable. Sure, I could mix some sugar with carbonated water and try to sell it to you, but you are probably going to opt for a Coke because you know what to expect.

The quantitative and qualitative factors we covered are really just scratching the surface—for a deep dive on applying these concepts to find undervalued and overlooked companies, I strongly recommend you check out the recommended readings listed in chapter 7. You may end up being the next Warren Buffet if you have a knack for picking stocks!

At the end of the day, there are no clear indicators, equations, or graphs than can be drawn to let you know whether a stock selection will pan out with 100% certainty. Still, many value investors advocate that with a lightly diversified group of companies (10–15) with strong fundamentals, a self-selected portfolio can, over time, outperform even the best mutual fund money manager.

One approach could be to try half of your portfolio in the "Portfolio Focus Strategy" (performing your own research and selecting your own stocks) and half in the "Diversification Strategy" (buying into ETFs and/or placing a set amount of money into a highly rated mutual fund). See what works for you. Ultimately, because you can easily match the broader market by investing in an ETF or mutual fund, you should judge your portfolio versus the S&P 500. If the S&P 500 has risen 8% in the past year, but your account performance is just at 3%, it may be best to take a step back and shift some money away from individual stocks and into an index-tracking ETF or mutual fund. Remember that 9.7% average annual return we mentioned earlier? Your goal is to match or beat it, no less.

## Things to Think About

1. Would mutual funds, ETFs, or the Portfolio Focus Strategy (or a combination of the three) be best for you? Are you leaning more toward the "hands-off" approach of investing in mutual funds and ETFs, or does the idea of performing your own research for the more "hands-on" Portfolio Focus Strategy excite you?
2. What company makes your dream car? If you search for that company's stock chart online, can you pick out the market cap, EPS, and P/E ratio?
3. Thinking of your favorite brands of clothing, sports equipment, or tech, what qualitative advantages do they have to increase sales? Why are they better than their competition? What convinced you to want to buy those products?

# CHAPTER 5

# A STEP-BY-STEP GUIDE TO GETTING STARTED

Now that you know *why* you should start saving now, *what* type of account to open, and *where* to put your money, I am going to show you *how*. Time to put all this reading into action!

Not long ago, investors like you and I used to have to physically walk into a bank or dial an actual live agent to "place a trade" and purchase shares of stock. With the advancement of technology, this process has been made much easier. It can all be done online, and even via apps on your cell phone. During market hours, shares can be purchased instantly with the click of a button. There are many online platforms to choose from when you open your account, and they are called "brokerages." A broker is a matchmaker for investors—they bring together buyers and sellers and facilitate the trade between the two. A brokerage *account* allows you to buy and sell your investments. Sample platforms as of this writing include E*TRADE, Fidelity, Vanguard, and Charles Schwab. Make sure the brokerage you are using carries Roth IRAs! Some do not.

When researching brokerages to determine the route you want to take, make sure to compare commissions (fees for buying or selling stock, which are usually charged as a flat rate per order). As of this writing, many brokerages are moving to a commission-free model for stocks and ETFs. Zero-fee trades are becoming the new industry standard. You can find the latest by browsing their different websites to get familiar—obviously, the cheaper the fees the better. Some brokerages that still do charge commissions justify this because they offer more options for technical analysis for more complicated (and more active) trading strategies. For buy-and-hold investing (which is advocated for retirement savings) and for beginners, a commission-free brokerage will likely suffice.

## Opening an Account

Here is the step-by-step process for opening an account through an online brokerage. Click "Open an Account" on their homepage. The whole process should not take more than fifteen minutes. Exact details will differ depending on the brokerage you use, but the general flow of the application will look something like this:

1.  Account Selection

    You will need to choose an account type. The Roth IRA option will most likely be listed with other retirement account options. See chapter 3 where this is discussed. Make sure you select the correct one!

2.  Personal Information

    Input your general personal details, such as full name, phone numbers, email, and physical address.

3.  Identity Verification

    You will need your Social Security number to open an account. And if you are under age eighteen, most brokerages will require you to open a "Custodial" account, which means you will need a parent's or guardian's Social Security number in place of yours.

Technically, they will have ownership of the account on your behalf, until you turn eighteen, at which point it will rollover to your name. If this is the case, your parents will also need to input their marital status, number of dependents, occupation, annual income, and net worth on the application. Your parent(s)/guardian(s) may be skittish about doing this (mine were). Encourage them to read this chapter or search for more information online if they must. This may be the single greatest favor they ever do you.

4.  Account Login

    Now that the account is opened, you will be prompted to create a username and password to log in with. Build a strong password that is unique to this account and keep it somewhere safe.

5.  Name Beneficiaries

    Most platforms will require you to set beneficiaries, to define who should receive your money if you have an untimely death. Uncomfortable to think about, but necessary. You will likely need to provide their Social Security numbers and birthdates to list them. If listing more than one person, you can usually split out which percentage of your total funds you want to go to each person. Welcome to the world of "adulting."

6.  Investing Goals

    Many applications will have you fill out a section on your investing goals, to get a feel for what you are trying to accomplish with your new account. Answer however you think, but do not worry about listing anything incorrectly on this part; it is not terribly pertinent to the setup of your account.

7. Funding

> Finally, link your checking/savings account and transfer some money in (most will not require a minimum initial deposit, but it depends on the brokerage; this would rarely be more than $500). Once your first contribution is deposited and cleared (this can take a week or so, depending on the platform you use), the time has come to make your first trade!

If you have a steady source of income, consider setting up recurring contributions (once you log in to your account, this will usually be listed in the tab for "Transfers"). Your brokerage will then automatically draft your bank account every month (or every two weeks, or every week, etc.) on the dates you select. For example, if you want to contribute a total of $2,400 for the year, then set up a monthly contribution of $200 ($200 x 12 months = $2,400 total).

Also consider "turning on" your brokerage's "dividend reinvestment" option. They go by different names depending on the brokerage, but they all perform the same action—they reinvest your dividend payments. Remember those dividend payments we discussed in chapter 2? Enrolling in a Dividend Reinvestment Plan (DRIP) will automatically take your dividend disbursements and invest them commission-free into additional shares of the same stock (oftentimes buying partial shares of the stock), as shown in figure 9. Instead of letting that cash sit idle in your account, why not just reinvest it? More compounding!

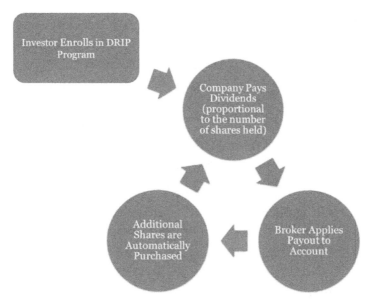

Figure 9: Dividend Reinvestment Plan—Simplified

## Placing an Order

Assuming you already know which stock(s) and/or funds you want to own (see chapter 4), you now need to decide how many shares to buy. A relatively easy thing to calculate, simply divide the total amount you wish to put into the company by the most recent stock price. Note that share prices are an ever-moving target, even in the after-hours markets, but usually you will not see any changes too drastic from the time you place the order to the time it gets filled. Do not fret; there is a way to tell your broker the maximum price that you are willing to pay.

If you are putting money into a mutual fund, simply search for the fund you want, click "Buy" and input your desired investment amount, and then click "Place order." It is really that simple.

There is a little more to it if you are placing an order for an ETF or for individual shares of stock. First, from your account, search for the company/ETF name and pull up its summary page. Click "Buy" to take you to the order form. Here, you will see the "Last Price" listed, which is the price per share. Divide the total amount of money that your wish to invest into the company/ETF by the "Last Price." This will give you the "Quantity" of shares for you to input. If your broker does not offer fractional trading (the ability to buy portions of a share), you will need to round up or down to the nearest whole number of shares.

Next, you will need to select a "Price type" (or "Order type"), which will let your broker know what price you are willing to pay for the shares. Do not be intimidated by the different options you see, which will probably look something like this:

**Market**—buy ASAP at the best available price

**Market on close**—buy as a market order as close as possible to the close of trading on the day the order is entered

**Limit**—buy only at a specific price or better (this is how you tell your broker the maximum price that you are willing to pay)

**Stop on quote**—once your specified price is reached, a market order is executed, and the entire order is filled at the best available price

**Stop limit on quote**—once your specified price is reached, a limit order is triggered to buy only at a specific price or better

The most commonly used option here is "Market," and this is all you will likely ever need to select. However, if for some reason you determine that there is a maximum price that you are willing to pay per share, and you do not want the order to be executed unless it is below that price, then it would be best to place a "Limit" order. "Stop" orders are used when you want to wait for the stock to reach a certain price before executing the trade. I rarely use Stop orders.

Once your price type is selected, you will likely need to specify a "Duration" for the order, which will tell your broker how long you want it to remain in effect, until fully executed or canceled. For example, you may be able to select "Good for day," "Good for 60 days," or even "Good until date," and then put in your specific end date. If your price-type criteria are not met by market close on the end date, the entire order will be canceled. I most commonly place "Good for day" orders. We're not trying to get fancy here! Once this info is entered, you should be able to complete the purchase.

Congratulations! You are now an owner of whichever companies you have invested in. You will reap the benefits of each business's success. Become an advocate for the companies you own! Purchase their products in place of their competitors' products, wear their brands, and help spread awareness of their names. In the next chapter, we will highlight steps you can take to avoid some common pitfalls for beginner investors.

## Things to Think About

1. Do you have any friends with an existing investment account whose broker would give either of you a referral bonus for opening a new Roth IRA?

2. Do you have a stable-enough income stream from work that will allow you to set up recurring transfers into your new account? Would a monthly or quarterly alarm be helpful in reminding you to login and buy more stock each time you have more cash to contribute?

# CHAPTER 6

## AVOIDING PITFALLS

---

H ave you ever bought something at the mall, only to regret the purchase one week later? We call this "buyer's remorse," and it happens to the investment community as well. We often get this feeling when our emotions are deeply intertwined in the buying process. As a result, serious investors are constantly reminding themselves to keep all emotion off the table when trading stocks. In fact, many of the common pitfalls that I will list here can be classified as "emotional investing."

### Pitfall 1—Panic Selling

To be a successful long-term investor, you will need to be able to stomach short-term losses. On average, over time, a diversified portfolio representative of the broader market will go up. It always has. Still, sometimes it will go down (sometimes dramatically), and your account balance will decrease. You will see all the major indexes dropping (DOW, S&P 500, NASDAQ, etc.), the headlines will report record lows each day, and economists all over the news will spout fiscal catastrophe. Do not sell. It is a tale as old as time. Stay invested and keep contributing. Many studies have shown that investors are better off staying in the market through the good times and the bad.

If the market is pulling back, and the S&P 500 chart is dropping lower day after day (what is referred to as a "Bear market"), chances are you can get some pretty good deals on valuable companies. You may want to even con-sider increasing your contributions during this time. Be wary though; it is not recommended that you withhold contributions to your account just because it seems like the market is headed down. This is called "timing the mar-ket" when you think you can wait and buy stocks at a better price later, and it is a dangerous mindset. This brings us right to our second pitfall.

## Pitfall 2—Inconsistent Contributions

History shows us that consistent purchases of invest-ment assets, throughout the highs and the lows of the market, is the best practice for buy-and-hold investors. Do not stop  contributing. Put some money in every month, or every paycheck— as much as possible. If you have a big purchase coming up or need to make payments for col-lege, fine. Just do yourself a favor and skip the midnight fast-food run, or better yet the $200 concert tickets. Put it toward your future instead. Every. Single. Month. Remind yourself of the Cheeseburger Rule from chapter 1.

This will likely be the most difficult hurdle to over-come for a teenager. Consciously giving up experiences and material possessions now, to save for the future, will require not only motivation but discipline. It will certainly require more spending discipline than your peers, and of-tentimes more discipline than your parents and friends' parents, and all the other adults in your life. If it were easy to tame the urge to spend money, many more people would be millionaires.

In line with the recommendation to maintain consistent contributions, many experts support following the "Dollar Cost Averaging" method when purchasing investments. With this concept, instead of investing all of your available cash for the year as a lump sum on one single day, spread it out a little—month by month or week by week. This will help you avoid entering the market at a very high price. Remember, you want to buy as cheaply as possible. You can average out the day-to-day swings and volatility of the stock market by investing little by little at set intervals. When you look back after having invested the total amount you intended, you will usually find that you have lowered your overall cost basis (average price paid), therefore providing you a better return.

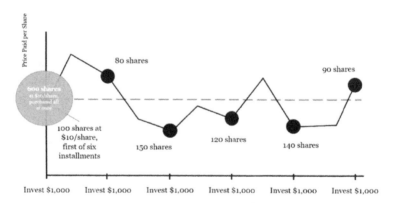

Figure 10: Implementation of Dollar Cost Averaging

Imagine you have $6,000 that you want to invest into a company, which is currently priced at $10 per share. You have two options. You can either (1) invest all $6,000 at once or (2) use Dollar Cost Averaging to invest equal amounts at spaced-out time intervals. Figure 10 compares the two scenarios on a timeline. If you place all $6,000 of your money into the investment today, you will own 600 shares at a fixed price of $10 each. *Or* you can place only $1,000 of your money into the investment today, and then continue doing the same thing every couple of months until you have spent all $6,000.

Throughout the year, the stock price will likely sometimes be above $10/share, and sometimes below. As the stock price goes up, your $1,000 investment amount does not go as far (it buys you less shares). As the price goes down, though, you get more "bang for your buck." In the hypothetical example in figure 10, your six different purchases would result in you owning 680 shares (versus 600) at an *average* price of $8.82 each. For the same total investment amount, the Dollar Cost Averaging method allowed you to end up owning more shares because it lowered your cost basis.

Keep in mind that if your broker charges commission on each trade that you make, the added fees each time you make a separate order will eat away at the benefits of Dollar Cost Averaging. Fortunately, the new "zero-fee" trading model of most brokerages will likely not cause an issue for you. Still, this is an excellent segue to our third pitfall— paying high fees.

## Pitfall 3—Paying High Fees

The biggest mistake I ever made when I started investing in the stock market was paying too much in fees. I overdiversified. This was back in the day when order commissions were more common in brokerages, and they were $9.99 per order on the platform I was using. I found myself putting $100 into each company I wanted to own, but because the fee just to *purchase* the investment was almost ten bucks, I was losing 10% on my investment right off the bat! That is like an entire year's worth of growth, gone immediately. Fees are always worth looking into.

My own example highlights the need to be aware of (and avoid) order commissions, but you should also pay attention to any fees imbedded in the funds you purchase. This does not apply to individual stocks, but instead when you buy into an ETF or a mutual fund. These all have management fees (also known as the "expense ratio"). As of this writing, the average expense ratio of all ETFs is 0.44% but can range as low as 0.03% and as high as 1.0%. A 0.44% expense ratio would mean that owning the fund would cost you $4.40 in fees for every $1,000 that you have invested into it, each year. Compounded over time, these fees get very pricey and can take a sizeable chunk out of your retirement fund.

Most mutual funds are more "actively managed," so the fees are higher. The managers are constantly swapping out shares of one company for another, to beat the market. However, on average, over time, many mutual funds usually do not beat the broader market indexes, but the fees they charge sure make it seem like they do. Please do not get me wrong—there are some mutual funds out there that put out returns that make the management fees worth it, but you must be careful. The average expense ratio of a mutual fund as of this writing is around 0.79% but can range from 0.5% to 2.5%. Some mutual funds also charge a one-time fee when you buy into it (called the "load"), but there are many "no load" options available as well.

As alluded to, unfortunately, the magic of compounding applies to fees as well, and the magnifying effect is incredible (figure 11). For example, a 1% annual expense ratio on a $10k investment can reduce your total returns by almost 17% after twenty years of compounding! This gap widens even farther as you increase the time frame. How about we consider our example from chapter 1: $6,000 per year contributed into an account returning 9.7% annually, from age eighteen to retirement at age sixty. If the investment funds in this account charge a 0.44% expense ratio, you lose over $440,000 to fees. At an expense ratio of 0.79%, you lose over $750,000 to fees. Ignoring fees when picking investments is a huge mistake.

| Account Balance on $10k Initial Investment (10% annual return) | | | | | | | | | |
|---|---|---|---|---|---|---|---|---|---|
| Year | 0% Expense Ratio | | 0.5% Expense Ratio | | 1.0% Expense Ratio | | 1.5% Expense Ratio | | 2.0% Expense Ratio |
| 0 | $ | 10,000 | $ | 10,000 | $ | 10,000 | $ | 10,000 | $ 10,000 |
| 1 | $ | 11,000 | $ | 10,950 | $ | 10,900 | $ | 10,850 | $ 10,800 |
| 2 | $ | 12,100 | $ | 11,990 | $ | 11,881 | $ | 11,775 | $ 11,668 |
| 3 | $ | 13,310 | $ | 13,129 | $ | 12,950 | $ | 12,780 | $ 12,610 |
| 4 | $ | 14,641 | $ | 14,375 | $ | 14,116 | $ | 13,874 | $ 13,632 |
| 5 | $ | 16,105 | $ | 15,739 | $ | 15,386 | $ | 15,064 | $ 14,742 |
| 6 | $ | 17,716 | $ | 17,233 | $ | 16,772 | $ | 16,360 | $ 15,947 |
| 7 | $ | 19,487 | $ | 18,867 | $ | 18,281 | $ | 17,769 | $ 17,254 |
| 8 | $ | 21,436 | $ | 20,657 | $ | 19,927 | $ | 19,304 | $ 18,675 |
| 9 | $ | 23,579 | $ | 22,614 | $ | 21,720 | $ | 20,973 | $ 20,217 |
| 10 | $ | 25,937 | $ | 24,758 | $ | 23,676 | $ | 22,791 | $ 21,894 |
| 11 | $ | 28,531 | $ | 27,104 | $ | 25,808 | $ | 24,770 | $ 23,714 |
| 12 | $ | 31,384 | $ | 29,672 | $ | 28,131 | $ | 26,925 | $ 25,693 |
| 13 | $ | 34,523 | $ | 32,483 | $ | 30,666 | $ | 29,273 | $ 27,843 |
| 14 | $ | 37,975 | $ | 35,558 | $ | 33,427 | $ | 31,828 | $ 30,179 |
| 15 | $ | 41,772 | $ | 38,924 | $ | 36,438 | $ | 34,611 | $ 32,718 |
| 16 | $ | 45,950 | $ | 42,608 | $ | 39,722 | $ | 37,643 | $ 35,480 |
| 17 | $ | 50,545 | $ | 46,639 | $ | 43,302 | $ | 40,946 | $ 38,482 |
| 18 | $ | 55,599 | $ | 51,050 | $ | 47,204 | $ | 44,544 | $ 41,746 |
| 19 | $ | 61,159 | $ | 55,877 | $ | 51,460 | $ | 48,464 | $ 45,296 |
| 20 | $ | 67,275 | $ | 61,159 | $ | 56,100 | $ | 52,736 | $ 49,157 |
| Lost to Fees | | | $ | (6,116) | $ | (11,175) | $ | (14,539) | $ (18,118) |
| % Overall Return Lost to Fees | | | | -9.1% | | -16.6% | | -21.6% | -26.9% |

Figure 11: The Effects of Fees on Compounded Investments

To simulate the impacts of fees on your investments, there are several ETF and mutual fund screeners available online. You can search by name, category, or industry and compare expense ratios across similar funds. The goal here is to make *yourself* rich, not some fund manager on Wall Street. Do your own research, empower yourself with knowledge, and skip the fees.

## Pitfall 4—FOMO

The "Fear of Missing Out" (FOMO) is an all-too-real emotion that works its way into every investor's head. When we see a stock's price skyrocket 50% in one day, we get this feeling. You say to yourself and your friends, "Stock ABC is going to the moon! It just keeps going higher and higher. Don't get left behind!" Try not to get caught up in the hype, because what goes up, must (usually) come down. Even the stock market cannot evade the laws of gravity.

This advice mostly applies to investors who plan on selecting their own individual stocks for their portfolio, not mutual fund and ETF investors. Heavily diversified funds will not usually see daily price swings large enough to induce the feeling of FOMO investing.

Take Webvan.com as an example. Webvan, an online grocery store, was one of the largest flops during the dot-com bubble of the late 1990s. Webvan promised to deliver to customers within a thirty-minute window of their choosing, prompting them to build extremely expensive warehouses in many American cities. Webvan went public in 1999 via an "initial public offering" and skyrocketed up to $34 a share during intraday trading due to investor sentiment—a 65% increase from the initial offering price. The stock then plummeted to only pennies a few months later, and by 2001, Webvan was bankrupt (figure 12). They burned through more than $800 million in investor funding. The company failed, and the early investors who got caught up in the hype lost everything. Perhaps Webvan had the right idea (think Amazon.com) but had an unproven business model and were a little ahead of their time.

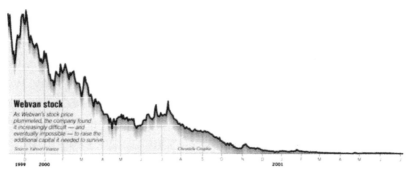

Figure 12: The Decline of Webvan Stock (*SF Gate*)

Heavily traded stocks with continuous price increases day after day are most likely going to experience a "correction" at some point, which will lower the price quickly. Even if the increased price movement seems to be warranted by, say, an unexpected new product launch or winning a big government contract, excitement can quickly get out of control. Buying the stock at an all-time high may not be the best decision. You do not want to be left holding the bag when the floor drops.

"Be fearful when others are greedy and greedy when others are fearful." —Warren Buffet

## Pitfall 5—Following the "Experts"

Up to this point in your life, you have likely been told that your elders are always right. I am here to tell you they are not—especially those on Wall Street!

Across the financial industry, bloggers, gurus, and money managers advertise themselves as experts at predicting stock movements. They all claim to have figured out the key to unlocking riches in the stock market. Many of these folks have good intentions, but a large portion of them are scammers trying to take your money. Either way, not ONE person knows which direction a stock is headed tomorrow, any more than you or I do. (Okay, some people may have insider information, but it is illegal to trade stocks based on insider info. We rely on the US Securities and Exchange Commission to keep this in check.)

The batting averages of most financial "analysts" are quite low when we compare their past predictions to historical performance. Why? Because to correctly predict a stock's increase or decrease in price, you have to first correctly predict all of the factors that can affect it: government policy, economic direction, supply and demand, interest rates, foreign politics, and all new technological inventions. Simply put, you must predict the future, or at least own a time machine. Best of luck!

As supporting evidence to this, a 2016 Dalbar study showed that for the thirty-year period ending December 31, 2015, the S&P 500 index produced an annual return of 10.35%, while the average equity mutual fund investor earned only 3.66% (figure 13). There are some good money managers out there, but on average they struggle to keep pace or outperform the broader market, which can instead be tracked with lower-fee passive ETFs.

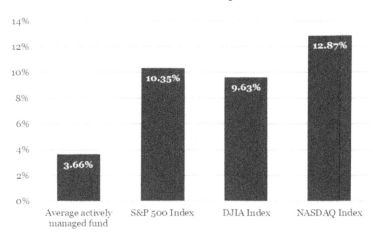

Figure 13: Average Annual Returns based on
Historical Performance (1985–2015)

63

This should feel empowering as a teenager. Steer clear of the experts claiming the next big thing. Instead, do your own research, consider the use of the Diversification and Portfolio Focus strategies we discussed, invest with a buy-and-hold, long-term mindset, and have history on your side. You have all the information available in front of you to beat the adults at their own game.

To be clear, just because we should stay away from those with strategies for the short term, there are still some fabled investors to whom we should pay some respect and heed their advice. The long-term investment strategies they have laid out formed the basis for much of this book. Our last chapter will list out some of these recommendations for further reading.

# CHAPTER 7

## RECOMMENDED READINGS

---

K nowledge is power. Knowledge is also money, as many before us have realized. I hope that this book arms you with the motivation, as well as a sufficient foundation, to start investing for retirement without any further delay. In addition, it would be prudent to seek out supplementary reading material to continue your learning. Follow in the footsteps of legendary investors with these recommended readings.

*The Intelligent Investor: The Definitive Book on Value Investing* by Benjamin Graham

Widely considered the founder of value investing, Benjamin Graham will provide you with all the info you need to properly execute stock-picking for the Portfolio Focus Strategy. This book lays out the strategy for determining a business's financial worth based on intrinsic value for buy-and-hold long-term investing and also provides a deeper dive into what numbers and ratios you should consider. It gets dense but offers a very thorough introduction to investing. Graham mentored modern investing icon Warren Buffett.

*The Essays of Warren Buffett: Lessons for Corporate America* by Warren Buffett

Speaking of Warren Buffett, you will want to learn as much as possible from this guy. I have quoted him a bit in earlier chapters, and while he sometimes goes against the grain of others in the investment community, Buffett certainly has the track record to deserve respect. As tenured CEO of Berkshire Hathaway, Buffett has guided the fund's growth to far outpace the S&P 500. Buffett specializes in picking out companies with strong growth potential—at bargain prices. Much of his investing philosophy is captured in the annual letter he writes to Berkshire Hathaway shareholders. These letters have since been compiled into a book and are surprisingly easy for beginner investors to follow.

*The Little Book of Common Sense Investing: The Only Way to Guarantee Your Fair Share of Stock Market Returns* by John Bogle

In earlier chapters, we discussed the importance of keeping fees low when buying into a mutual fund or ETF. John Bogle was certainly passionate about this topic. He revolutionized investing for retail investors like you and me when he invented the "index fund" in 1975. This leveled the playing field by providing us with a market-tracking investment vehicle with adequate diversification, while at a much lower cost than those high-fee mutual funds. Eventually, this concept morphed into the present-day ETFs. His book goes into detail on why high fees will significantly reduce returns.

*The Total Money Makeover: A Proven Plan for Financial Fitness* by Dave Ramsey

This book is in its own lane, separate from the investing books shared previously. I have it listed here because I still think it is applicable for getting in the necessary mindset to build your financial future. A good portion of the book is focused on debt avoidance and elimination, which may not be applicable to you now (you may need to revisit this after college graduation), but the book also emphasizes smart money habits that are crucial to develop as soon as possible. The budgeting tactics that Ramsey proposes are foolproof for building a strong savings ethic, and he shows ways to keep spending in check so that you can invest as much of your income as possible.

# Conclusion

# Invest Hard Now, Play Hard Later

I hope that you have learned a few things by reading this book. For many, the confidence required to open your own investment account and enter the stock market may not be achieved by reading a single book but by gathering information from several different sources— and that is okay. This is your personal financial journey, and it will not be the same as mine. Nor will it be the same as your parents'. At the very least you now have an idea of how the stock market operates, and hopefully you are empowered with the foundational knowledge to complete your own research on the investment options out there.

Perhaps most importantly, I hope that you now understand how critical it is that you *start investing early*. Compounded returns are to an investor as a hammer is to a handyman—the most important tool in the toolbox. While you cannot change or predict movements in the stock market, you can certainly control your investments' time in the market, which, as evidence shows, has the greatest impact on your portfolio's performance. Remember, a fourteen-year delay in saving could cost you up to $2.5 million at retirement. You simply cannot afford to wait.

The stock market is capitalism's gift to you. The average person does not have the credit or the capital to build wealth through real estate or start their own business. By investing in the stock market, you need nothing more than an online account to own any public company in the world and generate wealth through them. You do not have to be an expert stock picker or math wiz to build an investment portfolio worth millions. You simply need to start saving early, plan your investment strategy, and contribute as much money as possible on a consistent basis. At a young age, this will not come without sacrifice, reprioritization, or patience.

As I once heard a great cook say, "Do you want it to be done fast? Or do you want it to be done well?" The same concept applies to finances. Do you want a little bit of money now? Or do you want a hell-of-a-lot more money later?

You gave up personal time to read this book—now you must take it one step further to put everything in action. Maybe you already have a job and are raking in some earned income to fund your new account. If you do not, then it is time to start hustling. You may also need to cut back on your current spending habits; start by looking at your expenses on social events—there are so many free ways to spend quality time with your friends.

Additionally, there are likely several uncertainties present in your life at the moment. What college will I get accepted into? What will all my friendships look like after I graduate? Where will I end up living? What subject do I really want to major in at college? What career could I see myself working in? Is my current significant other going to work out? Despite all these reservations, there is one certainty you can count on: the constantly narrowing window for your savings to grow. Take action now to let your money make you money.

All of this effort is actually *for* something, of course. How will we play hard later? Well, this will look different for every person. What would you do with a few million dollars in your bank account? Buy a couple of vacation homes? Treat yourself to your dream car? Sponsor a cause you are passionate about? Take your loved ones on a trip around the world? How to spend your money is something only you can decide, but I am sure you will have a blast.

The clock is ticking...what else are you waiting for? Time to lock in your future wealth.

# KNOWLEDGE CHECK

1. What has been the average yearly growth rate of the total stock market since the early 1900s?
    a. 4.7%
    b. 2.0%
    c. 19.1%
    d. 9.7%

2. What are the two primary ways that being a stock owner can pay off?
    a. Increase in the price of stock & tax write offs
    b. Increase in the price of stock & income from dividend payments
    c. Free merchandise & income from dividend payments
    d. Income from dividend payments & tax write offs

3. Of the investment options listed below, which is the lowest risk/lowest reward?
    a. Bonds
    b. Individual Stocks
    c. Savings Accounts
    d. Mutual Funds

4. Which of the following statements is FALSE for a Roth IRA?
    a. There is no minimum age to qualify
    b. It allows for pre-tax contributions
    c. Money deposited must be earned income
    d. There is a yearly contribution limit

5. Which of the following are TRUE for both mutual funds and ETFs?

    a. Basket of many investments

    b. Offer diversification

    c. Charge fees (have an expense ratio)

    d. All of the above

6. What is the name of the brokerage account setting that will take your dividend payments and use them to buy more shares of stock?

    a. Dividend Reimbursement Plan

    b. Dividend Reinvestment Plan

    c. Dividend Diversification Plan

    d. Dividend Distribution Plan

7. Which market capitalization size meets the definition of a "small-cap" business?

    a. $10 billion or more

    b. $2 billion to $10 billion

    c. $300 million to $2 billion

    d. Less than $300 million

8. When you use a trading platform to purchase shares of a stock or ETF, you will need to select a "Price Type." Which of the following price types will *only* execute at a specific price or better?

    a. Market

    b. Market on Close

    c. Limit

    d. Stop on Quote

---

Want to find out how you did? Visit **investnowplaylater.com/worksheets** for the Answer Key. There, you can also download and print free copies of this knowledge check!

# ON YOUR MARK, GET SET, INVEST!

If you want to help your younger siblings start their investing journey, consider sharing this book with them!

**Scan**
to view on
**Amazon.com**

Geared for kids ages 8 to 12, *On Your Mark, Get Set, Invest!* provides over a dozen interactive worksheets, fun illustrations, and kid-friendly examples to simplify the essential concepts of money management and personal finance...many of which are not taught in schools.

Readers will get to learn from the money decisions of Ritzy Rabbit and Thrifty Tortoise as they race to the finish line—at the end awaits a brand-new bike!

# ACKNOWLEDGMENTS

There are many people whose support directly—and indirectly—helped this book become a reality.

I mostly owe thanks to my father, Eric, who first inspired me to learn about the stock market while I was in middle school. One might assume he was a businessman or corporate highflier with aspirations for his teenage son to live up to. However, he was a law enforcement officer in small-town Louisiana who taught me to make the most of my money, and who had a desire for his children to one day be financially free. This book would never have come to be without his encouragement. Not only did he teach me to constantly strive for self-betterment but to also have pride in my work. I am very proud of this book.

I also give thanks to my mother, Peggy—for teaching me that if I do something, I should do it right—and for my siblings, Anna and Jane, the two most supportive sisters an older brother could ask for.

Several friends and family members read the manuscript draft and offered great suggestions. They, just as importantly, also pretended to enjoy the topic.

- To Andrew LeBlanc: Since we became best friends in elementary school, no one has ever been able to criticize my work like you can—I know you'll take that as a compliment.
- To Jacques Bienvenu: I always fancied the idea of having a brother...now I have one (in-law) that is just as interested in the stock market as I am!

- To Austin Branch: Thanks for taking a break from becoming *Tik Tok* famous to help me revise this book.
- To Jane Villermin: You crucially helped me make this more relatable to teens (PS you really aren't that clumsy).
- To Aunt Ellen: Ever since we were roommates during my summer internship (when you gave feedback on my college papers), I knew you would be perfect for helping me to shape this story.

Lastly, for Avery Cooper, my "Alpha" tester, thank you so much for sticking by my side throughout this writing process, keeping me motivated, and allowing me to bounce ideas off you. Your input was immensely helpful, and I have the coolest cover artwork because of you!

# ABOUT THE AUTHOR

Luke Villermin opened a retirement account and started investing in the stock market at fifteen years old. His only regret...he didn't start earlier. Since then, he has become the best-selling author of the *Invest Now Play Later* series and has shared his investing knowledge on multiple podcasts and interviews.

When he isn't working his corporate day job or advocating financial literacy for young people, you can find him hiking, camping, and traveling to new places.

Visit his website at lukevillermin.com. He loves to hear from readers.

# FULL DISCLAIMER

The data and scenarios in this text are approximations and have been presented for the purpose of proving a point. Past stock/mutual fund/ETF performance is not indicative of future performance.

It is important to remember that these scenarios are hypothetical, future rates of return cannot be predicted with certainty, and investments that pay higher rates of return are generally subject to higher risk and volatility. The actual rate of return on investments can vary widely over time, especially for long-term investments. This includes the potential loss of principal on your investment. It is not possible to invest directly in an index, and the compounded rate of returns referenced in this text do not reflect sales charges and other fees that investment funds and/or investment companies may charge.

The information provided in this book is for informational purposes only and is not intended to be a source of advice or credit analysis with respect to the material presented. The information and/ or documents contained in this book do not constitute legal or financial advice and should never be used without first consulting with a financial professional to determine what may be best for your individual needs.

The publisher and the author do not make any guarantee or other promise as to any results that may be obtained from using the content of this book. You should never make any investment decision without first consulting with your own financial advisor and conducting your own research and due diligence. To the maximum extent permitted by law, the publisher and the author disclaim any and all liability in the event any information, commentary, analysis, opinions, advice, and/or recommendations contained in this book prove to be inaccurate, incomplete, or unreliable or result in any investment or other losses.

Content contained or made available through this book is not intended to and does not constitute legal advice or investment advice, and no attorney–client relationship is formed. The publisher and the author are providing this book and its contents on an "as is" basis. Your use of the information in this book is at your own risk.

Did this book help you in some way?
Please leave an honest review online so
that others can find it as well!

**Scan below to be directed to the
Amazon.com review submission page:**

Your feedback is much appreciated. Thank you.

Made in the USA
Monee, IL
25 July 2023